First published in Great Britain in 1997 by
Brockhampton Press,
20 Bloomsbury Street,
London WC1B 3QA.
A member of the Hodder Headline Group.

This series of little gift books was made by Frances Banfield, Penny
Clarke, Clive Collins, Jack Cooper, Nick Diggory, John Dunne, David
Goodman, Paul Gregory, Douglas Hall, Lucinda Hawksley, Dicky
Howett, Dennis Hovell, Helen Johnson, C. M. Lee, John Maxwell,
Patrick McCreeth, Morse Modaberi, Sonya Newland, Anne Newman,
Terry Price, Mike Seabrook, Nigel Soper, Karen Sullivan, Nick Wells
and Matt Weyland.

ISBN 1 86019 559 8

A copy of the CIP data is available from the British Library upon
request.

Produced for Brockhampton Press by Flame Tree Publishing, a part
of The Foundry Creative Media Company Limited, The Long House,
Antrobus Road, Chiswick, London W4 5HY.

Printed and bound in Italy by L.E.G.O. Spa.

Just For You
GET WELL SOON

Illustrated by

Douglas Hall

A.R.C.A.

Selected by Karen Sullivan

BROCKHAMPTON PRESS

You're a regular wreck, with a crick in your neck,
and no wonder you snore,
for your head's on the floor, and you've needles
and pins from your soles to
your shins, and your flesh is a-creep, for your left
leg's asleep, and you've
cramp in your toes, and a fly on your nose, and
some fluff in your lung, and a
feverish tongue, and a thirst that's intense, and a
general sense that you
haven't been sleeping in clover.

But the darkness has passed, and it's daylight at
last, and the night has
been long — ditto, ditto my song — and thank
goodness they're both of them
over!

W. S. Gilbert, 'A Nightmare'

It's no longer a question of staying healthy. It's a question of finding a sickness you like.
Jackie Mason

When I was kept lying in bed
With an ache in my heart and my head
My knees made high hills
To hide biscuits and pills
Under books which I still haven't read.
Jane Whittle

I'm for anything that gets you through the night, be it prayer, tranquillisers or Jack Daniels.
Frank Sinatra

My corns
ache, I get
gouty and my
prejudices swell like varicose veins.
James Gibbons Huneker

A hospital is a place where people who are run
down generally wind up.
Anonymous

And just about *everybody*

gets measles,

mumps,

and chickenpox

sometime or other.

They don't always come at the handiest time.

They might interfere with Christmas or birthdays

or the circus,

BUT

once you have had them, you almost certainly will

never have them again.

So

Have a happy measle, a merry mumps, a cheery

chickenpox, and grin and bear whatever else

comes along.

Jeanne Bendick, 'Have a Happy Measle, Have a Merry Mumps,

Have a Cheery Chickenpox'

If you find a dullness, heaviness and weariness after food, or a proneness so soon as you have eaten, be sure you have taken too much; for meat and drink ought to refresh the body and make it cheerful, and not oppress it and make it dull.

Culpeper

I got the bill for my surgery. Now I know what those doctors were wearing masks for.

James H. Boren

What have I gained by health? Intolerable
dullness. What by early hours and moderate
meals? A total blank.

Charles Lamb

Medicine is the only profession that labours
incessantly to destroy the reason for its own
existence.

James Bryce

Strive to preserve your health, and in this
you will the better succeed in proportion as
you keep clear of the physicians.

Leonardo da Vinci

When people's ill, they come to I,
I physics, bleeds, and sweats 'em;
Sometimes they live, sometimes they die.
What's that to I? I let's 'em.

John Coakley Lettsom

Everyone who is born holds dual citizenship, in
the kingdom of the well and in the kingdom of
the sick.

Susan Sontag

Health indeed is a precious thing, to recover and
preserve which we undergo any misery, drink
bitter potions, freely give our goods: restore a man
to his health, his purse lies open to thee.

Robert Burton, *Anatomy of Melancholy*

When I was sick and lay a-bed,
I had two pillows at my head,
And all my toys beside me lay
To keep me happy all the day.
Robert Louis Stevenson, 'The Land of Counterpane'

Joy and Temperance and Repose
Slam the door on the doctor's nose.
Henry Wadsworth Longfellow

Oh to be a broken leg
In plaster white as chalk
And travel everywhere by
crutch
While others have to walk.
Mike Griffin

A specialist is a doctor whose patients are expected to confine their ailments to office hours.
Anonymous

Our body is a machine for living. It is organized for that, it is in its nature. Let life go on in it unhindered and let it defend itself, it will do more than if you paralyse it by encumbering it with remedies.
Leo Tolstoy, *War and Peace*

Pine is the 'tree of peace' of the Native American Iroquois. Burn it to purify the home, and decorate its branches to bring healing and joy.

Never go to a doctor whose office plants have died.
Erma Bombeck

I don't deserve this award,
but I have arthritis and I don't
deserve that either.
Jack Benny

Mary had a little lamb,
A lobster and some prunes,
A glass of milk, a piece of pie,
And then some macaroons.

It made the busy waiters grin
To see her order so,
And when they carried Mary out,
Her face was white as snow.

Anonymous

That poor people such as work hard, and fare
hard, and are seldom idle, have more children,
and those stronger and lustier of body, are
usually longer lived than those that live idly
and fare deliciously.

Culpeper

That it may please thee to preserve all that travel by land or by water, all women labouring of child, all sick persons, and young children.

The Book of Common Prayer

Three out of four doctors recommend another doctor.

Graffito

It occurred to me that there was no difference between men, in intelligence or race, so profound as the difference between the sick and the well.

F. Scott Fitzgerald

The whole imposing edifice of modern medicine is like the celebrated tower of Pisa — slightly off balance.

Charles, Prince of Wales

Measure your health by your sympathy with morning and spring. If there is no response in you to the awakening of nature — if the prospect of an early morning walk does not banish sleep, if the warble of the first bluebird does not thrill you — know that the morning and spring of your life are past. Thus may you feel your pulse.

Henry David Thoreau

Quit worrying about your health. It'll go away.
Robert Orben

❖

There was a faith-healer of Deal,
Who said, 'Although the pain
isn't real,
If I sit on a pin
And it punctures my
skin,
I dislike what I fancy I
feel.'
Anonymous

❖

Health and cheerfulness
mutually beget each other.
Joseph Addison

Health is not a condition of matter, but of mind.
Science and Health

❖

Fresh shamrocks are placed in the sickroom to bring health and healing; the dried leaf is said to protect the heart from diseases.

❖

Of all the anti-social vested interests the worst is the vested interest in ill-health.
George Bernard Shaw

❖

Health is my expected heaven.
John Keats

He had had much experience of physicians, and said, 'the only way to keep your health is to eat what you don't want, drink what you don't like, and do what you'd druther not.'

Mark Twain

Natural forces within us are the true healers of disease.

Hippocrates

Lavender
in the home
brings
peace, joy
and healing.

Country lore

Before undergoing a surgical
operation, arrange your temporal
affairs. You may live.

Ambrose Bierce

I suppose one has a greater sense of intellectual
degradation after an interview with a doctor than
from any human experience.

Alice James

Show me a sane man and I will
cure him for you.

C. G. Jung

Better to hunt in fields, for health unbought,
Than fee the doctor for a nauseous draught.
The wise, for cure, on exercise depend;
God never made his work for man to mend.

John Dryden

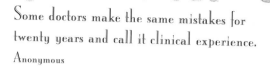

Some doctors make the same mistakes for twenty years and call it clinical experience.

Anonymous

One must not forget that recovery is brought about not by the physician, but by the sick man himself. He heals himself, by his own power, exactly as he walks by means of his own power, or eats, or thinks, breathes or sleeps.

Georg Groddeck

It is better to lose health like a spendthrift than to waste it like a miser.

Robert Louis Stevenson, *Virginibus Puerisque*

Health is not valued until sickness comes.

Spanish proverb

My heart aches, and a drowsy numbness pains
My sense, as though of hemlock I had drunk,
Or emptied some dull opiate to the drains
One minute past, and Lethe-wards had sunk:
'Tis not through envy of thy happy lot,
But being too happy in thine happiness, —
That thou, light-winged Dryad of the trees,
In some melodious plot
Of beechen green, and shadows numberless,
Singest of summer in full-throated ease.

John Keats, 'Ode to a Nightingale'

O who can tell
The hidden power of herbes and might of
Magick spell?
Edmund Spenser, *The Faerie Queene*

You're a born loser if you take a four-way cold
tablet and find you have a five-way cold.
Leopold Fechtner

It is part of the cure
to wish to be
cured.
Seneca

To eat an apple going to
bed
Will make the doctor beg
his bread.
Traditional

One knows so well the popular idea of health. The
English country gentleman galloping after a fox —
the unspeakable in full pursuit of the uneatable.
Oscar Wilde

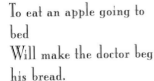

'Tis healthy to be sick sometimes.
Henry David Thoreau

Culture is what your butcher would have if he
were a surgeon.
Mary Pettibone Poole

He who was never sick dies of the first fit.
English proverb

Cardiologists don't really need to give stress tests
and EKGs. They can check the condition of a
patient's heart just by sending him a bill.
Anonymous

Deep peace I breathe into you.
O weariness, here:
O ache, here!
Deep peace, a soft white dove to you;
Deep peace, a quiet rain to you;
Deep peace, an ebbing wave to you!
Deep peace, red wind of the east from you;
Deep peace, grey wind of the west to you;
Deep peace, dark wind of the north from you;
Deep peace, blue wind of the south to you!
Deep peace, pure red of the flame to you;
Deep peace, pure white of the moon to you;
Deep peace, pure green of the grass to you;
Deep peace, pure brown of the earth to you;
Deep peace, pure grey of the dew to you,
Deep peace, pure blue of the sky to you!
Deep peace of the running wave to you,
Deep peace of the flowing air to you,
Deep peace of the quiet earth to you,
Deep peace of the sleeping stones to you,
Deep peace of the Yellow Shepherd to you,

Deep peace of the Wandering Shepherdess to you,
Deep peace of the Flock of Stars to you,
Deep peace of the Son of Peace to you,
Deep peace from the heart of Mary to you,
And from Bridget of the Mangle,
Deep peace, deep peace!

Celtic blessing of peace and healing

To be sick is to enjoy monarchical prerogatives.

Charles Lamb

35

Attention to health is the greatest
hindrance to life.
Plato

⬦

Medicinal discovery,
It moves in mighty leaps,
It leapt straight past the common cold
And gave it us for keeps.
Pam Ayres, 'Oh No, I Got a Cold'

⬦

Balm is sovereign for the brain, strengthening the
memory and powerfully chasing away melancholy.
John Evelyn

⬦

Diseases are the tax on pleasures.
John Ray

Mummy, I love you. I hope you get well soon.
William, 5

Borage and hellebore fill two scenes
Sovereign plants to purge the veins
Of melancholy, and cheer the heart
Of those black fumes which
make it smart.
Robert Burton

It is my joy in life to find
At every turning of the road
The strong arm of a comrade kind
To help me onward with my load.
Frank Dempster Sherman

The cure for this ill, is not to sit still,
Or frowst with a book by the fire;
But to take a large hoe and a shovel also,
And dig till you gently perspire.
Rudyard Kipling, 'How the Camel Got His Hump'

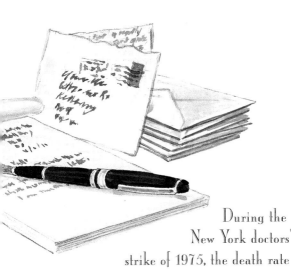

During the New York doctors' strike of 1975, the death rate fell by more than 15 per cent.

Now when a doctor's patients are perplexed,
A consultation comes in order next —
You know what that is? In a certain place
Meet certain doctors to discuss a case
And other matters, such as weather, crops,
Potatoes, pumpkins, lager-beer, and hops.
Oliver Wendell Holmes, Sr

Illness is not very nice.

Freddie, 6

An old Norfolk remedy for children's
health: sew them into their
clothes in the autumn
and don't release
them until the
spring.

I wish healing upon you,
The healing of Mary with me,
Mary, Michael and Brighid
Be with me all three.

Your pain and sickness
Be in the earth's depths,
Be upon the grey stones,
For they are enduring.

Fly with the birds of the air,
Fly with the wasps of the hill,
Swim with the sea-going whale,
For they are swiftest.

Be upon the clouds of the sky,
For they are the rainiest,
Be upon the river's current
Cascading to the sea.

Celtic blessing of healing

According to studies I have made, elders enjoy much better health than most people think they do. For example, Bruce Bliven, at age 79, wrote: 'I have calculated that the diseases I don't have outnumber those I have by twenty to one, so I am only 5 per cent ill.' However, a 77-year-old man wrote to me: 'I seem to be in good health though getting out of bed in the mornings makes the raising of Lazarus look like a cheap trick.'

A Treasury of Humour

You can say 'Get Well Soon' if someone is ill.
Alex, 5

You aren't ill: it is just that you are made of second-rate materials.
Natalia Ginzburg

Sickness sensitizes man for observation, like a photographic plate.
Edmond and Jules de Goncourt

As a cure for the cold, take your toddy to bed, put one bowler hat at the foot, and drink until you see two.
Sir Robert Bruce Lockhart

Dearest Lord, may I see you today and every day in the person of your sick, and, whilst nursing them, minister unto you. Though you hide yourself behind the unattractive disguise of the irritable, the exacting, the unreasonable, may I still recognize you, and say: 'Jesus, my patient, how sweet it is to serve you.'

Mother Teresa

If you have leprosy, you really really must say 'Get Well Soon'.

Pria, 5

With any recovery from morbidity there must go a certain healthy humiliation.

G. K. Chesterton

The doctor learns that if he gets ahead of the superstitions of his patients he is a ruined man; and the result is that he instinctively takes care not to get ahead of them.

George Bernard Shaw

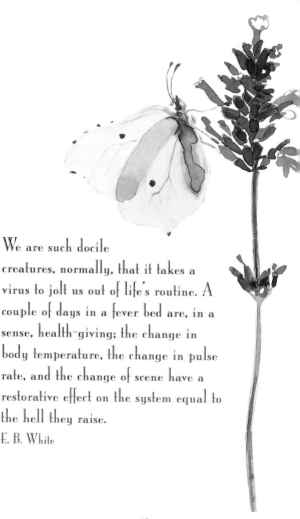

We are such docile creatures, normally, that it takes a virus to jolt us out of life's routine. A couple of days in a fever bed are, in a sense, health-giving; the change in body temperature, the change in pulse rate, and the change of scene have a restorative effect on the system equal to the hell they raise.

E. B. White

My doctor gave me six months to live but when I couldn't pay the bill, he gave me six months more.

Walter Matthau

What I call a good patient is one who, having found a good physician, sticks to him till he dies.

Oliver Wendell Holmes, Sr

You know you're not well when in the morning you hear snap, crackle, pop, and it isn't your breakfast cereal.

Anonymous

I have noticed that doctors who fail in the practice of medicine have a tendency to seek one another's company and aid in consultation. A doctor who cannot take out your appendix properly will recommend you to a doctor who will be unable to remove your tonsils with success.

Ernest Hemingway

Bride went out
One morning early,
With her two horses;
One broke its leg
With much ado.
What was apart
She put together
Bone to bone,
Flesh to flesh,
Sinew to sinew,
Vein to vein;
As she healed that
May we heal this.

Celtic blessing to heal a sprain or any disunity

When I had a swollen ankle, I got a Get Well Soon thing.

Cole, 5

How many desolate creatures on the earth
Have learnt the simple dues of fellowship
And social comfort, in a hospital.

Elizabeth Barrett Browning

Tell me how much
you know of the
sufferings of your
fellow men and I will
tell how much you
have loved them.

Helmut Thielicke

Take anything any doctor says with a grain of aspirin.
Goodman Ace

I enjoy convalescence. It is the part that makes the illness worthwhile.
George Bernard Shaw

God speaks to us in our joy but shouts to us in our pain.
Anonymous

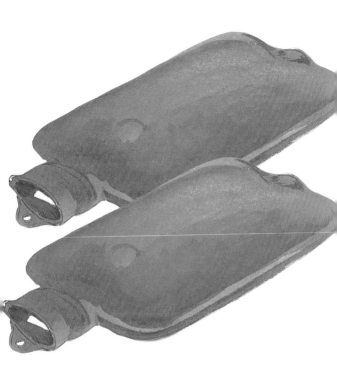

Treasure the love you receive above all. It will survive long after your gold and food and health have vanished.

Og Mandino

Before the girls could believe the happy truth, the doctor came to confirm it. He was a homely man, but they thought his face quite heavenly when he smiled, and said, with a fatherly look at them, 'Yes, my dears; I think the little girl will pull through this time. Keep the house quiet; let her sleep, and when she wakes give her — '

What they were to give, neither heard; for both crept into the dark hall and . . . held each other close, rejoicing . . . .

Louisa May Alcott, *Little Women*

A friend should bear his friend's infirmities.

William Shakespeare

The best way to get a doctor to make a home visit is to marry him.

Anonymous

I reckon being ill is one of the great pleasures of life, provided one is not too ill and is not obliged to work till one is better.

Samuel Butler

How good it feels — the hand of an old friend.

Henry Wadsworth Longfellow

If you start to think about your physical or moral
condition, you usually find that you are sick.
Johann Wolfgang von Goethe, *Proverbs in Prose*

How sickness enlarges the dimension of a man's
self to himself!
Charles Lamb

My Doctor is on the Golf Diet —
he lives on greens.
Anonymous

It doesn't breathe;
It doesn't smell;
It doesn't feel
So very well.
I am discouraged
With my nose:
The only thing it
Does is blows.

Dorothy Aldis

The best cure for hypochondria is to
forget about your body and get
interested in somebody else's.

Goodman Ace

Medical science says that whiskey can't cure the common cold, but neither can medical science.

Anonymous

Had she found Jane in any apparent danger, Mrs Bennet would have been very miserable; but being satisfied on seeing her that her illness was not alarming, she had no wish of her recovering immediately as her restoration to health would probably remove her from Netherfield.

Jane Austen, *Pride and Prejudice*

On a healthy autumn day . . . weak but otherwise restored, [he] sat listening to a voice that read to him. On a healthy autumn day; when the golden fields had been reaped and ploughed again, when the summer fruits had ripened and waned, when the green perspectives of hops had been laid low by the busy pickers, when the apples clustering in the orchards were russet, and the berries of the mountain ash were crimson among the yellowing foliage . . . listening to the voice as it read to him, [he] heard in it all that great Nature was doing, heard in it all the soothing songs she sings to man.

Charles Dickens, *Little Dorrit*

Acknowledgements:

The Publishers wish to thank everyone who gave permission to reproduce the quotes in this book. Every effort has been made to contact the copyright holders, but in the event that an oversight has occurred, the publishers would be delighted to rectify any omissions in future editions of this book. Children's quotes printed courtesy of Herne Hill School; Susan Sontag reprinted courtesy of *The New York Review of Books*; George Bernard Shaw reprinted courtesy of the Society of Authors, on behalf of the estate of George Bernard Shaw; Rudyard Kipling reprinted courtesy of Macmillan Publishers Limited; Celtic blessings translated by John and Caitlin Matthews, appearing in *The Little Book of Celtic Wisdom* and *The Little Book of Celtic Blessings*, reprinted courtesy of Element Books; P. G. Wodehouse extracts © P. G. Wodehouse, reprinted courtesy of Herbert Jenkins and Penguin Books; E. B. White reprinted courtesy of Hamish Hamilton Children's Books and Harper & Row Publishers Inc.; *A Treasury of Humor*, by Eric W. Johnson, published by Ivy Book, Ballantine Books © Eric W. Johnson, 1989; *5000 One and Two Line Jokes*, compiled by Leopold Fechtner © Parker Publishing Company Inc., 1973.